The C at Number 9

Jonny Zucker

Illustrated by
Steve Horrocks

OXFORD
UNIVERSITY PRESS

OXFORD
UNIVERSITY PRESS

Great Clarendon Street, Oxford, OX2 6DP,
United Kingdom

Oxford University Press is a department of the University of Oxford.
It furthers the University's objective of excellence in research, scholarship,
and education by publishing worldwide. Oxford is a registered trade mark of
Oxford University Press in the UK and in certain other countries

Text © Jonny Zucker 2017

Illustrations © Steve Horrocks 2017

The moral rights of the author have been asserted

First published 2017

All rights reserved. No part of this publication may be reproduced, stored
in a retrieval system, or transmitted, in any form or by any means, without
the prior permission in writing of Oxford University Press, or as expressly
permitted by law, by licence or under terms agreed with the appropriate
reprographics rights organization. Enquiries concerning reproduction outside
the scope of the above should be sent to the Rights Department, Oxford
University Press, at the address above.

You must not circulate this work in any other form
and you must impose this same condition on any acquirer

British Library Cataloguing in Publication Data
Data available

978-0-19-837772-6

3 5 7 9 10 8 6 4

Paper used in the production of this book is a natural, recyclable product
made from wood grown in sustainable forests. The manufacturing process
conforms to the environmental regulations of the country of origin.

Printed in China by Leo Paper Products Ltd.

Acknowledgements
Inside cover notes written by Karra McFarlane

Contents

1 Save the Park! 5
2 Inside Number 9 11
3 In Disguise 19
4 Boms Wants Food! 26
5 The Squirrel Search 34
6 Time's Running Out 41
7 The Great Party 49
8 A Proper Park 57
About the author 64

Chapter 1
Save the Park!

"I think we designed these leaflets pretty well," said Keesha, shielding her eyes from the hot sun.

Nick adjusted the bag on his shoulder and looked at a leaflet.

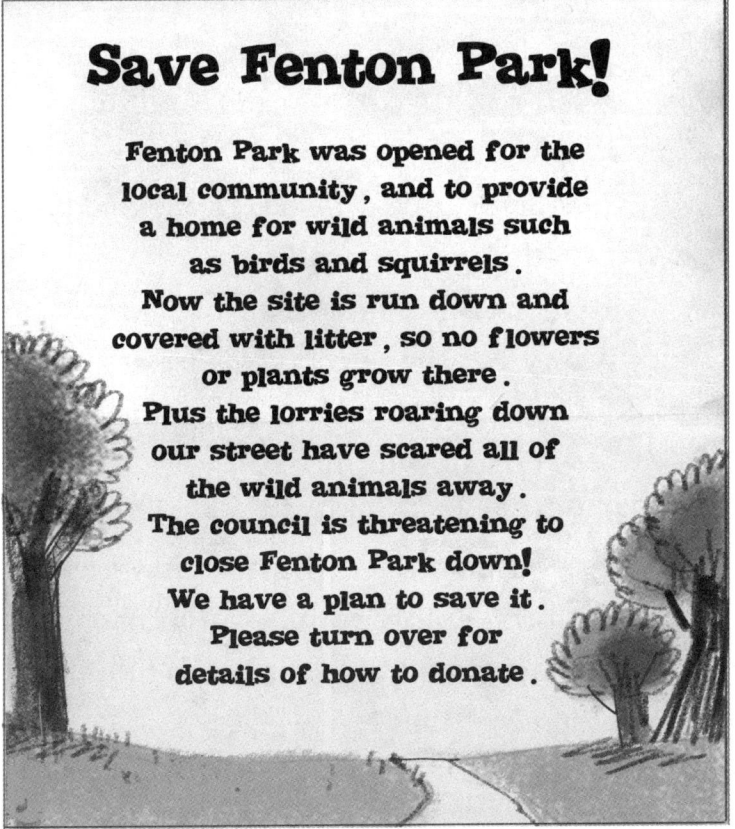

Save Fenton Park!

Fenton Park was opened for the local community, and to provide a home for wild animals such as birds and squirrels.
Now the site is run down and covered with litter, so no flowers or plants grow there.
Plus the lorries roaring down our street have scared all of the wild animals away.
The council is threatening to close Fenton Park down!
We have a plan to save it.
Please turn over for details of how to donate.

"I hope they work," said Nick. "We all used to play at Fenton Park but now it's like a rubbish dump."

"There used to be a gardener but the council won't pay her any more," said Keesha. "If we collect loads of money, at least we could pay a team of people to clear away the litter."

"And the wild animals – like the squirrels and rabbits and deer – have all been scared off by the lorries trundling down Fenton Road," added Nick.

"Come on," said Keesha. "Let's make a start with these leaflets."

Fifteen minutes later their bags were empty and Keesha and Nick were standing outside number 9 Fenton Road.

Keesha lived at number 7.

Nick lived at number 11.

The house between them – number 9 – had been empty for years. For as long as they both could remember, no one had lived there.

The blinds were always down.
The curtains were always closed.
The lights were always off.

"Hang on a minute," frowned Nick, staring at number 9.

Keesha followed his gaze. "Wow!" she said. "There's a light on downstairs. Someone must have moved in!"

"Do you think we should post a leaflet through their letter box?" asked Nick. "I've got a spare one in my pocket."

"We *have* given one to every other house," said Keesha, scratching her cheek thoughtfully.

They took a couple of steps down the garden path.

"Listen," whispered Nick.

From inside the house came the sound of strange, low voices.

Keesha and Nick exchanged a nervous glance and took another few steps forward.

At an upstairs window a huge yellow eye appeared for a second, blinked twice and then disappeared.

"That wasn't like any eye I've seen before," gulped Keesha.

Nick shivered. "I'm not sure it's the kind of eye I want to meet."

They tiptoed up to the front door.

At that second there was a giant sneezing noise from inside and the whole house shook, like a tree in a violent thunderstorm.

Keesha and Nick jumped back in shock.

"Maybe we should just leave it," said Nick, glancing at his house next door. Suddenly he wanted to be safely tucked away inside it.

"If there are new people living here we should at least say hello and be friendly," said Keesha. "You know, ask them if they need a cup of sugar or something."

"I'm sure they've got their own sugar," said Nick.

"Come on," said Keesha, "it'll only

take a few seconds to introduce ourselves, and we can give them the leaflet at the same time."

"Couldn't we introduce ourselves from our own houses?" asked Nick.

"Don't be ridiculous!" scoffed Keesha.

Nick took a look at the upstairs window again. There was no sign of the huge yellow eye.

"OK," he said, slowly nodding his head.

Keesha reached out her hand. She grabbed the bronze door knocker, and knocked on the door.

Chapter 2
Inside Number 9

The door of number 9 wasn't locked, so it slowly swung open, making a loud creaking sound.

"Er ... hello?" called out Keesha.

There was no reply.

"Let's forget about it," said Nick, taking a few steps back.

"No," replied Keesha, sounding like a strict teacher.

Nick sighed and they crept inside, down a narrow hallway and into the living room. A gigantic box of blue popcorn rested on a table. A plant with strange purple flowers stood on the floor.

"Who eats blue popcorn?" Nick whispered.

They walked over to a window and looked into the backyard. There were several statues of giant creatures knitted in orange wool.

"Weird," muttered Nick.

They left the living room and headed to the kitchen. On a table sat two enormous uneven pink plates. There was a jug filled to the brim with a frothing green liquid, and a toaster with spaces for sixteen slices of bread.

"Maybe it's a family with lots of children," said Keesha.

"Or maybe whoever lives here just likes toast," said Nick.

At that moment they heard heavy footsteps clonking down the stairs. Nick grabbed Keesha by the elbow.

A few seconds later two giant figures entered the kitchen.

One was a woman.

She had a green body and huge yellow eyes. Her hair was in coils and at the end of each coil was the head of a light blue snake. The snakes were chatting and giggling with each other.

The other was a man. He was enormously tall and his body was icy white. He looked a bit like a giant upright sheep. He had a white beard and sunken blue eyes.

Keesha opened her mouth to scream. Nick held on to the table to stop himself falling over.

"Wait!" cried the woman. "I know we look frightening but we're actually really nice."

"Yeah," nodded the man. "I like knitting. I knitted the statues in the garden."

"Who … who … who are you?" Keesha managed to say.

"I'm Medusa," said the woman, "and this is the Abominable Snowman."

"But you can call us Med and Boms," grinned the Abominable Snowman, arranging sixteen slices of yellow bread in the toaster and taking a long glug from the frothing green jug.

"I thought you were only in legends," said Nick, hiding behind Keesha.

"Myths and legends? They're just like fairy stories – a pack of lies," huffed Medusa.

"For example, no one turns to stone just by looking at Med's face," said Boms. "And I don't chase people across vast plains of ice."

"W … w … what about your snakes?" asked Nick, nervously.

"These guys?" purred Med, tickling some of the snakes' heads and getting high-pitched laughter back in return. "They wouldn't hurt a fly."

"So what are you doing on Fenton Road?" asked Keesha, stepping forward and gently stroking one of the snakes.

"We keep getting moved on," replied Boms. "Wherever we go, people see us and start screaming and then we're asked to go to another area. Anyone for toast?"

Sixteen burned yellow slices popped out of the toaster and Boms caught them all in one of his huge hands.

"Er ... no thanks," said Nick.

"Well, let us introduce you to our parents and our neighbours," said Keesha. "If we say you're OK, then they'll just have to accept you."

"No way," said Med. "We've tried being friendly with adults before but it never works."

Boms yanked open the fridge and stared at its empty shelves. "Rats," he sighed, "we're out of mud jam."

"We need more food," said Med. "We always make our own but we can't seem to find any of the right ingredients around here."

"And if we go out in daylight and someone sees us, they'll probably call the police," added Boms.

"I'd probably call the police," murmured Nick.

"Wait," said Keesha, her face lighting up. "I have an idea."

"What kind of idea?" asked Boms.

But Keesha was already halfway out of the kitchen.

Chapter 3
In Disguise

Five minutes later, Keesha was back, carrying armfuls of clothes.

"I borrowed these from my mum and dad," she panted, piling the clothes on the kitchen table.

"You'll be in big trouble if they find out," said Nick.

"They won't find out," said Keesha. "Now come on!"

It only took a few moments to dress up Med and Boms.

Boms wore one of Keesha's dad's suits (it was way too small but somehow he managed to squeeze into it). He also wore sunglasses and a golfing cap.

Med wore Keesha's mum's green dress and a purple bobble hat that covered up all of her snakes.

"You both look great," beamed Keesha.

"You both look almost human," nodded Nick.

"I'm so hungry I could eat a human," sighed Boms.

Keesha and Nick stared at him in horror.

"I'm only joking," he grinned.

"So these leaflets you were posting," said Med. "What are they about?"

The four of them had been walking for a while and were almost at the shops. So far, no one who had passed them had screamed or called the police.

"They're about the park behind our houses," explained Keesha. "The council is saying they will send someone to inspect it. If it's still full of rubbish and no wild animals live there, they'll close it down."

"But if we can raise some money and pay someone to clear up all of the litter, and pay a gardener to get some flowers and plants growing ..." said Nick.

"And stop the heavy traffic pounding down Fenton Road so some of the wild animals come back," added Keesha, "we may be able to save it."

"We've written to the council twice about the lorries but they never replied," said Nick.

Keesha sighed. "Here's the mini supermarket," she said.

"Great," said Boms, rubbing his freezing hands together.

A few minutes later, Med and Boms were looking down in the dumps.

"They don't have any of the food we're used to," sighed Med.

"Yeah," nodded Boms. "There are no rock sandwiches or dust lollies."

"Lots of the food here is really tasty," said Nick, trying to cheer them up.

"If you like, we could choose some food and cook it for you," said Keesha, grabbing a basket and throwing a packet of spaghetti into it.

"Yes," agreed Nick, chucking a packet of tomatoes into the basket. "My dad's a great cook so I know loads of recipes."

"I suppose that might work," said Med, "just don't use too much sugar. Boms has a really sweet tooth and he eats far too much rubbish."

"You sound like my mum," Nick groaned.

By the time they'd chosen everything they wanted, the basket was pretty full. The woman behind the counter packed everything into two bags and Med got out her purse to pay.

She'd just handed over a couple of notes when the hat on her head started to slip off.

Keesha saw this and quickly tried to grab it and push it back. But it slid past her fingers and on to the floor.

In a flash all of the snakes on Med's head were revealed. The woman behind the counter opened her mouth as if she wasn't sure whether to scream or call the police.

Chapter 4
Boms Wants Food!

"It's OK," shouted Keesha, snatching the hat off the floor and shoving it back on to Med's head. "She's … she's in a play!"

"It's about Medusa," cried Nick.

"She's got the main part," added Keesha.

The woman's shocked face suddenly broke into a smile. "*I'm* in a drama group," she said. "In the last play I got the part of a chair."

"Maybe you'll get a table or something bigger in the next one," said Nick, taking the shopping bags and hurrying the others out of the shop.

"Phew, that was close," said Boms, as they started making their way back to Fenton Road.

"You saved the day," said Med, patting Keesha on the back.

"No problem," smiled Keesha.

As soon as they returned to number 9, Nick got busy in the kitchen. Packets were prised apart, tins were opened, herbs were sprinkled.

"That doesn't smell like any food I've ever eaten before," said Med, her snakes hissing warily.

"I present to you, spaghetti with fresh tomato sauce," announced Nick with a bow. He brought four steaming bowls to the kitchen table.

"Try it," said Keesha. "You'll love it!"

Boms gave Med a nervous look. Med gave Boms an anxious glance. Med twiddled her snakes in her fingers.

Med sighed, then grabbed a large handful of spaghetti and sauce in her fist and dropped it into her mouth. She chewed and thought and chewed some more, and then she smiled. "This is good!" she nodded.

Boms took a mouthful and spat it out. "Yuk!" he cried. "That is the most disgusting thing I've ever tasted!"

"Boms!" tutted Med angrily.

"Sorry," he said guiltily, "but it's just not my thing."

"That's fine," said Nick. "I know plenty of other recipes. We'll find something you like. You could finish off that green juice stuff for now."

Boms nodded and glugged the rest of the frothing liquid.

"While I do the washing-up," said Keesha, "you three start thinking about ways we can introduce you to all of our neighbours without scaring people half to death."

"Good idea," nodded Nick, "the quicker people get to know you, the better."

By Thursday evening, Keesha and Nick's Fenton Park money collection consisted of one note and a few coins.

"This will never pay for a rubbish removal team," groaned Nick.

So they knocked on all of their neighbours' doors asking if they'd be willing to do some tidying up at the park.

Some people said no. Some people said maybe. Three people said yes.

Half an hour later, Keesha and Nick were down at Fenton Park, with Keesha's dad and two neighbours.

"Can you pass that rubbish bag please?" asked Keesha, standing waist-high in litter.

There were crisp packets, drink cans and yellowing newspapers everywhere. It looked like a vast sea of junk.

"Be careful of any sharp tin cans," called over Keesha's dad.

"I will," replied Keesha.

Keesha started picking up rubbish and stuffing it into the sack.

Nick groaned and reached for some damp cardboard boxes to put in his sack.

The five of them were there for over two hours. They stopped as the sun started going down.

Nick put his hands on his hips and looked around. "I don't believe it," he said. "We've been breaking our backs and all we've done is clear a tiny space."

"A tiny space is better than no space," said Keesha positively. But she could see what Nick was talking about. To sort this place out properly they'd need more than her dad and two neighbours. Maybe it was an impossible task?

Chapter 5
The Squirrel Search

"Keep your voices down!" hissed Keesha.

It was Friday afternoon after school. She, Nick, Med and Boms were heading for the stream beside the garages at the end of Fenton Road.

"There's a family of squirrels living by the stream," Nick whispered as they crept past some hedges. Med and Boms were wearing the outfits that Keesha had 'borrowed' from her parents.

"Why have we got all of this food?" asked Med, clasping an old cracker tin.

"If the squirrels are there, we can lay down a trail of food," Keesha explained.

"We can lead them to Fenton Park," said Nick. "If we leave more food for them there, then maybe they can set up a new home."

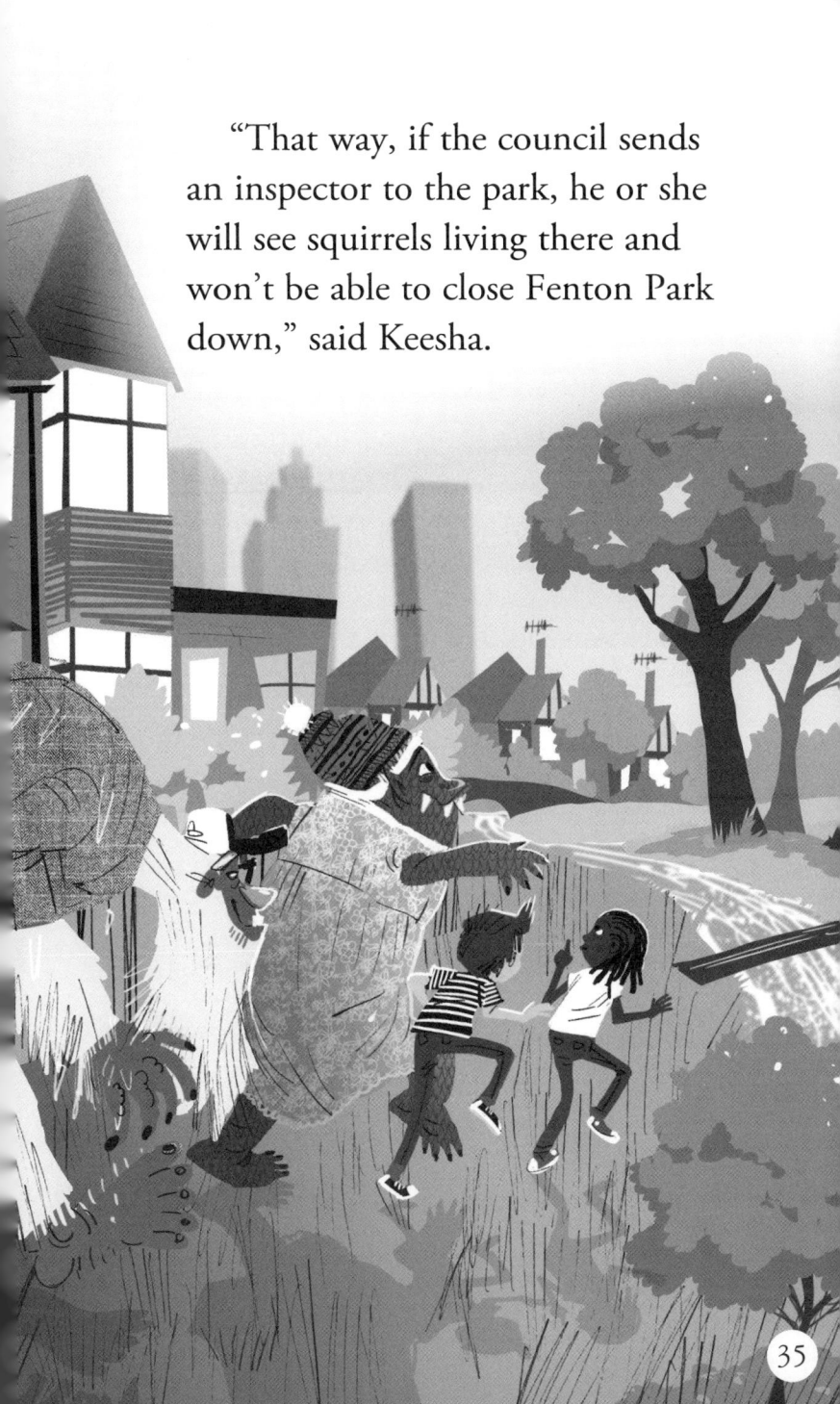

"That way, if the council sends an inspector to the park, he or she will see squirrels living there and won't be able to close Fenton Park down," said Keesha.

"Sounds like a great idea," nodded Boms, as they stole past the house on the corner and scurried along a passage that led down to the stream.

There was a pathway that ran the entire length of the stream, and at the side of that pathway was a long row of trees.

"Look," whispered Nick after a few minutes, pointing upwards. "We've struck gold!"

He was right. Up in one of the trees was a family of squirrels, their large eyes blinking, wary but unafraid.

"Crack open that tin," instructed Keesha.

Boms pulled open the lid and placed some old crackers down on the pathway. For a few moments the squirrels did nothing. But then one of the larger ones sniffed the air, scurried down the tree and took a few paces towards the food. It bent down, licked the corner of a cracker and then gobbled it up.

It looked over to its fellow squirrels and gave them some sort of signal. A few seconds later, they were all crowding around the crackers and enjoying a hearty meal.

Boms walked further along the pathway and put some more crackers on the ground. The squirrels waited a while and then made their way together towards this second mound of food. Before long they were chomping away at it too.

"It's working," cried Nick, "it's actually working!"

As the afternoon sun painted shadows across the gentle water of the stream, Keesha, Nick, Med and Boms laid a trail of more crackers, bits of raw spaghetti and breadcrumbs.

At the end of the pathway, they went over a bridge and down an alleyway that led to the entrance of Fenton Park.

"Once we get into the park, we'll put a large mound of food in the area that we cleared yesterday," said Nick.

They were within metres of Fenton Park when they heard a voice.

"Keesha, where are you?"

It was Keesha's mum.

"You haven't done your homework yet! You need to get home right now and make a start on it."

"Disaster!" groaned Keesha.

Chapter 6
Time's Running Out

"This way!" said Boms, grabbing Keesha and Nick's hands and charging back towards the alleyway and the stream. Med came racing along behind them.

"What about the squirrels?" demanded Nick.

He saw in despair that all of the squirrels were running back to their tree home beside the stream.

"It's too bad," replied Keesha.

Moving as fast as they could, they circled back to Fenton Road, avoiding Keesha's mum.

"Take these!" called Med, as she and Boms took off their borrowed clothes and chucked them to Keesha.

Nick and Keesha ran into their houses. Keesha raced upstairs and replaced all of her parents' clothes in their wardrobes. Then she dashed down again, and by the time her very confused mother returned home, Keesha was sitting at the kitchen table doing her homework.

On Saturday morning a very official-looking letter dropped through every letter box on Fenton Road.

Keesha's dad read the letter and when he'd finished his face was all frowns and seriousness.

"What is it?" asked Keesha.

"It's from the council," he replied. "It says we only have a week to save Fenton Park. They'll be sending an inspector down any time in the next seven days."

"Well I guess that's it then," said Keesha. "We'll never be able to clear it all up and reintroduce any wild animals there in that time."

"You never know," said her dad.

"Come on, Dad. You've seen how much work there is to do. And you know the council hasn't even replied to our letters about the lorries and traffic."

Keesha's dad said nothing.

On Saturday night Keesha and Nick popped over to number 9. They'd spent the afternoon with Keesha's dad at Fenton Park but once again they hardly had anything to show for their efforts. They were tired, frustrated and in very low spirits.

Med was at number 9, alone.

"Boms was complaining there's nothing to eat," Med informed them. "He's gone off in a huff."

"Did you see the letter from the council?" asked Nick.

"I'm afraid I did," nodded Med. "It doesn't seem fair only giving you seven days to sort the place out."

"It was a lovely dream to save it but I think we've just left it too late," sighed Keesha.

They sat in gloomy silence for a few minutes until an idea barged its way into Keesha's brain.

"Hey, I've just had a great idea," she said.

"Is it about how to clear up litter quicker and find a whole park full of wild animals in the next ten seconds?" asked Nick.

"No," said Keesha excitedly, "it's about how to introduce Med and Boms to everyone."

"Go on," said Med.

"You know your main problem is the moment people first see you, they scream or call the police?" said Keesha.

"Correct," nodded Med. "However hard we try to look friendly."

"So the way around it is to say that you look the way you do for a reason," said Keesha. Med looked puzzled.

"What we do is have a fancy dress party," said Keesha. "That way everyone will think that you're humans wearing dressing-up costumes. Once they've seen how you look and they're not scared, they won't *need* to be scared when we tell them that's how you look in real life."

"I like it," said Med, "but when would we hold the party?"

"Tomorrow," said Keesha.

Chapter 7
The Great Party

It took Keesha and Nick fifteen minutes to design and print the invitations. Then they dropped one through every letter box on Fenton Road.

> **Fancy dress lunch party tomorrow (Sunday).**
> **A great chance to meet your amazing new neighbours at number 9!**
> **Go wild with your costume and bring a dish.**

"If this works, at least it might make up a bit for Fenton Park being closed down," sighed Keesha.

Just as Keesha and Nick were about to leave number 9, Boms staggered in, looking totally exhausted, his belly bulging.

"Tummy ache," he complained, before hurrying upstairs and out of sight.

"Must have had too many slices of that yellow toast," remarked Nick.

"See you tomorrow," said Med, "and thanks for thinking of the party idea. It's fab!"

"Goodnight," said Keesha.

She and Nick reached the end of the path, high-fived and then went home. They had no idea what the next day might bring.

Sunday was a beautiful day. The sun shone down on Fenton Road and the blue sky stretched out like a huge oil painting.

At 11.55 am Keesha and Nick were standing in the hallway of number 9 with Med and Boms. All four of them were nervous.

"What happens if nobody comes?" said Nick.

"What happens if nobody brings a dish?" said Keesha.

But they needn't have worried.

As if by magic, as the clock struck twelve, front doors on the street started opening and people began streaming towards number 9, plates and bowls of food in hand.

It was incredible. By 12.15 pm the party was in full flow. Everyone was in fancy dress. There were cowboys and kings, trolls and space pilots, aliens and footballers.

"It's such a pleasure to meet you," someone was saying to Med. "Your outfit is the best I've ever seen. And those electronic snakes are so lifelike!"

"I can't believe how freezing your hands are," someone else was shouting at Boms, "and your beard is made of real ice. How very clever!"

There was so much food from so many different countries that you could eat all day long and never run out of new dishes to try.

"This is the best party I've ever been to," grinned Keesha, "and look how well people are getting on with Med and Boms!"

"It's brilliant!" nodded Nick. "We'll just have to time it perfectly when we tell people they're not wearing fancy dress."

Unfortunately, Keesha and Nick didn't get time to tell anybody anything. That was because Mrs Malford from number 44 wanted to examine the snakes on Med's head in detail. A split second after she touched them, they hissed at her and she screamed, "They're real! They're real!"

Once Mrs Malford started panicking, everyone else started too. It didn't take long for word to get around that Med and Boms weren't actually wearing fancy dress.

This led to lots of screaming and shouting and people rushing outside into the street.

"Wait!" yelled Keesha, running after everybody. "They may be real monsters but they're two of the nicest monsters you'll ever meet."

At that second a large brown council van roared down the street and pulled up with a screech of tyres just outside number 9. A man in a pinstriped suit climbed out. He looked very official and was wearing a badge.

Immediately all of the shrieking and wailing stopped.

"My name is Mr Frost and I am an inspector from the local council," said the man. "I am proceeding now to inspect Fenton Park. If it is totally covered in litter and there are no wild animals living there any more, then I will have no option but to shut it down."

He climbed back into his van and drove off down the street.

Keesha and Nick hadn't noticed that Med and Boms had slipped away.

"To Fenton Park!" shouted Keesha, sprinting down the street.

There were murmurs for a few seconds and then every single person took to their heels and raced after her.

Chapter 8
A Proper Park

Everyone arrived at Fenton Park a few moments after Inspector Frost got there.

People's mouths fell open and there were cries of shock.

All of the litter was gone. It was neat and tidy. Several bird feeders had been set up. Flower seeds had been planted. A woollen sculpture of a tree stood at each corner.

"What happened here?" Keesha gasped.

"It's not a mess at all," said Inspector Frost. "I was told it was a complete litter dump."

"So you'll let us keep it open?" asked Keesha.

"I'm afraid not," frowned the inspector. "There are no wild animals here."

"Are we wild enough for you?" asked Med, as she and Boms jumped down from a tree and started stomping towards the inspector.

He eyed them in horror and shrunk backwards.

"Was it you who got rid of the litter?" asked an amazed Nick.

Boms nodded. "I was hungry last night and I knew the junk needed clearing so I thought I'd kill two birds with one stone."

"That's why you looked so ill!" cried Keesha. "Your belly was full of rubbish."

Boms blushed and nodded, nursing his stomach.

Inspector Frost was still gaping at Med and Boms.

"W ... w ... well," he said, "it doesn't say anything about what *type* of wild creatures should be kept here."

"Exactly," said Nick. "And Med and Boms are *pretty* wild."

"The wildest," beamed Med. "In a good way, Inspector."

"There's another thing," said Boms. "Med and I aren't scared of big lorries but the other wild animals around here are." He eyed the inspector sternly.

"That's what made them go away in the first place," nodded Keesha. "All of that noise and pollution."

"So because you're an inspector at the council," said Med, taking a step towards the unfortunate man, "can you promise us that you'll ban all lorries from driving down Fenton Road?"

"Yes!" gasped Inspector Frost. "I'll make sure no lorries ever drive down Fenton Road again."

"How about vans and trucks?" asked Keesha.

"No vans or trucks or anything remotely bigger than a car," promised the inspector. "Now can I go?"

"Yes!" grinned Boms. "Have a nice day."

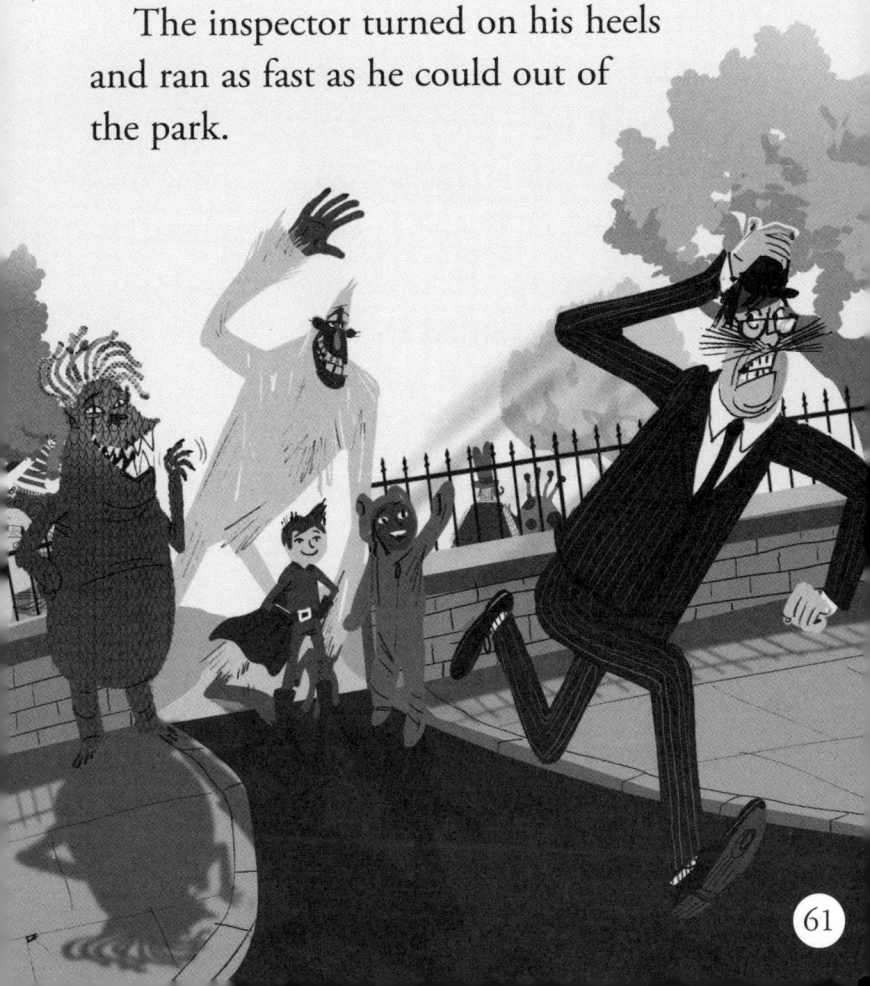

The inspector turned on his heels and ran as fast as he could out of the park.

"I'm so sorry," said Mrs Malford from number 44, giving Med and her snakes a pat. "I should have never judged you by the way you look."

"Do you knit?" asked Boms.

Mrs Malford nodded enthusiastically.

"Maybe we can swap knitting patterns?" said Boms.

"What a marvellous idea," grinned Mrs Malford.

"Look!" shouted Keesha.

Everyone fell silent as the family of squirrels peered around the entrance to the park and sniffed the air.

Keesha suddenly realized that she was still holding a piece of cake from the party. She put some crumbs on the ground. Very slowly, the squirrels began walking towards them.

"See," grinned Keesha. "Not only has the park just been saved, but wild animals are already back in it!"

Everyone started clapping.

The squirrels ignored the applause. They were much more interested in the cake crumbs.

About the author

As a child, I grew up near a park and I always loved to see the squirrels and foxes scampering about. As a grown-up author I decided to write a story about that park. I started thinking about what would happen if really big mythical creatures got involved in the story and that's when Med and Boms popped into my head! I now live near a different park and have my own kids, but so far we've never seen any creature that looks like Med or Boms – at least not yet!